SWEET MERCIES

poems by

Dianne Stepp

Finishing Line Press
Georgetown, Kentucky

SWEET MERCIES

Copyright © 2017 by Dianne Stepp
ISBN 978-1-63534-194-2 First Edition
All rights reserved under International and Pan-American Copyright Conventions. No part of this book may be reproduced in any manner whatsoever without written permission from the publisher, except in the case of brief quotations embodied in critical articles and reviews.

ACKNOWLEDGMENTS

Grateful acknowledgement is made to the editors of the following journals and presses for first publishing these poems or earlier versions of them.

Cider Press Review: "Crossing" (as "Mental Status Exam") and "Hunger"
Clackamas Literary Review: "What I know about war" and "Desecration" (as "Cutting up the Flag")
Comstock Review: "Birds, Probably Birds" and "After Camping"
Cries of the Spirit: "Filbert Orchard"
Elohi Gadugi: "Grief" and "Remodel"
Fireweed: "The arc of the moral universe" and "This Life"
High Desert Journal: "Up Canyon from Maupin"
TAMSEN: "Lazy Days" and "The Same Old Sky"
Windfall Press: "Winter Break at the Old Railroad Hotel" (as "Winter Break at the Old Lyle Hotel")

Many thanks to Judith Montgomery for her generous encouragement and advice, to the members of the Odds Poetry Group for their help with many of these poems, and, of course, to my dear husband, Mike Langtry, for his constancy and loving support.

Publisher: Leah Maines
Editor: Christen Kincaid
Cover Art: Barbara Adamson Sanders
Author Photo: Sandy Kennard
Cover Design: Elizabeth Maines McCleavy

Printed in the USA on acid-free paper.
Order online: www.finishinglinepress.com
        also available on amazon.com

        Author inquiries and mail orders:
        Finishing Line Press
        P. O. Box 1626
        Georgetown, Kentucky 40324
        U. S. A.

Table of Contents

- Remodel 1
- Hunger 3
- After an arctic wind and snow 4
- Crossing 5
- Settling Her Affairs 6
- Up Canyon from Maupin 8
- Dung 10
- Sweet Mercies 12
- After Camping 14
- Filbert Orchard 16
- Grief 17
- Winter Break at the Old Railroad Hotel 19
- Birds, Probably Birds 21
- The arc of the moral universe 22
- Lazy Days 23
- 1941:Escape 25
- View from the Porch 26
- What I know about war 27
- Desecration 29
- Already 30
- Coop 31
- This Life 32
- Arachnid 33
- The Same Old Sky 34
- Notes 35

Remodel

So they set the scream of the saw
into the old floor, pry out
the severed planks, releasing
into the torn house the dank
smell of dirt and mice.

Then the one with the swagger
and the tool belt slung low
on his hips slips through the opening
to call the measure of beams
and posts to the older two
squatting camp-style above him,

as though without understanding
how the floor could sink like that
without cracking the walls
they can't begin to fix it,
so take the point of this
and argue the level for that

until it seems to me the air
beyond the kitchen door
blooms with light, and an old Ford
idles at the edge of a clearing
near piles of planks and beams

scavenged from houses torn down
after the war, when the world
returned imperfectly to itself,
and making do was a virtue,
and patching over a necessity.
Twine marks the rows

where a young man in muddied bibs
paces the footings in spring soil.
A man for whom the only explosions
remaining are birdsong
rocketing down from the maples,
and the only fire leaps
in the tips of blood-red stems.

Hunger
> after *In Memory's Kitchen: A Legacy
> from the Women of Terezin*

They dream of yeast and goose fat, dough plaited to dough,
the old women of Theresienstadt.

Linzer torte, pirogen, goulash
with noodles.

Under the dead stars,
beside the stunned windows,

the blank belly of the stove.

They argue about hazelnuts in chocolate cake,
whether ground or chopped.

Whose version of coffee caramels.

From freezing bunks at night, they lament *Krieg*,
the food substitutes of war—

ersatz coffee, honey, egg optional in the strudel.

Someone calls for her favorite galantine of chicken,
garnished with caviar and paprika.

They press poems between the recipes. Letters,
Yahrzeit notes for the dead,

thread the pages to a book, hide it like a stolen loaf.

The daughter into whose hands years later
a stranger presses this parcel

trembles to touch it—

cries of apricot, apples, the small mouths of berries.

After an arctic wind and snow

shuts down the city,
and the white streets are empty,

and cars hunch at curb like stunned beasts,

we hike down the road to the nearby cemetery,
slip between the posts of the closed gate.

I walk behind, setting my feet in the crust of your footprints.

White caps fleece the granite gravestones,
and rime of crystal sets glaze to ornate scrolls and elegant serifs.

Caught unawares, the shrubs are brittle with fingers of ice,

and a shock of early robins scrabbles for berries
beneath a thicket of Ash.

As we loop and curve the shrouded lanes

braiding hillside and lawn,
I sense conversation interrupted, hands halted mid-gesture,

someone leaning against shovel or rake.

As if the marvel of snow beckons the dead
to the land of the living.

As if they climb from their tombs to prop their feet

on the stones, or gather in neighborly chats,
and hearing the crunch of our footsteps approach,

lift their hands to hail us as we pass.

Crossing

The doctor asks my mother
to name the season, but she looks
bewildered as to what a season is,
and as to day and month, only shrugs
her bird-like shoulders, although
when he asks the year,
she crosses her legs,
frowns, and without hesitation

announces the one decades ago
when my father left her, a landmark
she keeps in sight like those names
emblazoned on the side of a hill
in marigolds and purple petunias,
negative spaces bright with decorative
white pebbles, so she knows
where she is when she crosses
the border to a strange town.

Settling Her Affairs

When the radish seeds
I sow in neat rows
germinate sparsely,

or when the wrens peck out
the first sprouts,
leaving spindly white legs

shriveling in the sun,
it's almost a blessing.
Because when all the seeds

sprout at once, I can
almost hear them shrieking,
and then must kneel

to choose those few to let
live. And this is a lesson
my mother didn't teach me,

who saved the remaining
green stamps and empty
passbook to paste them in

that her sister collected sixty
years ago to trade
for two midnight-blue

China teacups glazed
with white pansies,
and a matching teapot,

all these years, still
unchipped. Inside
the bowl's dark eye,

the stain of black tea,
steeped on lazy
afternoons when a breeze

lifts a gauzy curtain,
and two young women
stir in sugar and cream.

Up Canyon from Maupin

We mill like strangers
by the river,
where the turbulence
spends itself in shallow licks.

The air is oily with juniper
and sage, the skeletal
rattle of weeds winter's only hint.

You carry the box of your dad's
ashes to a table under a willow,
your sister, the album.

Across the river a train
tears past. A breeze
catches your sister's hair,
twists a strand
to a button on your shirt.

*This is Virgil who loved fishing best.
Here he stands grinning
with his rod at his favorite hole,
hitching his waders.*

*Here are the scooped tail fins,
gash of gills laid in a row.*

*And here he holds to the camera
a hand-tied bucktail caddis fly.*

You read a poem about time
caught and locked in stone.
Your daughters look away,
perhaps embarrassed,
perhaps thinking of themselves

years hence, or thinking of the stars,
how they will hang
in dazzling clusters, how the moon
will alter the landscape to silver.

Someone finds a rock ledge
where the river plunges and bucks.
It takes the ashes slowly,
a milky swirl, a tail of white.

Dung

I've hauled so much of it
into my various yards
over the years—
elephant, bison, zebra
trucked from the zoo—
weekend trips to horse stables,
sheep farms, dairies.

And the time I drove
to the Mystic Lake Goat Farm
in the egg-blue square-back,
mine from the divorce,

and returned with seven gunny sacks
crammed with smelly shit
and a legion of fat flies
that circled and buzzed

all the way home, over the bridge
to the neat row of tidy houses,
mine tucked at the end,
where my squash plants waited
toed into mounds of hungry
urban dirt.

Blindly, without explaining
to myself, or even knowing
until now, that each time
I tilled a barrow of sweet
stinking muck into my own
thin patch, I repeated
the same ancient Braille
of gather, furrow, fallow

as those first women of the field,
stowing to sling, sack,
twist of skirt, from each
sacred animal

every clod, pellet, chip.

Sweet Mercies

It is Sunday afternoon, and we are driving
the same road we each drove

separately not many years ago.

I am bracing a mason jar of dahlias
and zinnias between my feet,

one orange dahlia nods against my knee,

and a yellow
zinnia caresses my calf.

Something about the dahlia's face,

its opulent gold petals,
puts me in mind of loneliness,

and I think of those local gods—
patrons of gardens and fruit trees,

minor deities with time on their hands

now so many orchards are sacrificed
to houses, and so few have time for gardens.

Suppose we were their lark, project or simple charity—

you attracting attention by virtue
of the lushness of your plums,

and I for the sweetness of my figs,

and because, both alone,
spading our separate plots,

soaking the roots of roses hottest days,

they recognized our loneliness,
and for this bruised their delicate hands

on the giant cogs and wheels,
the pulleys and levers of the universe,

edging you toward me, me toward you.

After Camping

Everything quiet so long
in the house, the carpet
without sound of our footfall,
windows without our gazes,
faucets, forgetting their water,
the bed, the shape
of our bodies.

This morning we watched
ravenous flocks of Townsend's Solitaires
storm the junipers—
pale yellow, dun, olive,
the birds were the camouflage
colors of everything—
the oily berries

they devoured, the boulder
that tabled our breakfast,
rabbit, deer, coyote,
nose down, the sly brush
of his tail.

We carry in the tent,
sleeping bags, pillows,
our weeks of dirty laundry,
making piles on the floor,
the counters.

How strange—on the table,
the bottle of oil I forgot,
yellowing on the sofa
last month's paper casually tossed—

as if the house held its breath
while we were gone,
as if it waited for the swoop
and dive of our hands

in the linens, for the rustle
in the bed clothes at night
as the shy animal of our twined lives
slips back to its haven.

Filbert Orchard

Limbs gnarled with lichen
they stagger in rows
down the hill. In spring
they sprout sparse flags,

wave them foolishly
at the jays. Moles
at their feet carve
generations of mansions.

Rotted and aging in place
they are those old fathers
we never had,
a company of lost men.

In the backyard at night,
bare feet on the Braille
of root and stone,
I hear them.

Brittle shiftings,
faint sounds like cries,
calls in the dark like at Vicksburg:

*Any of you boys
from Missouri? Seen my father?
My brother?*

Snow blankets the distant ridge,
sky hunkers down.
All that light.

Grief

Every day I walk fence,
tracing an invisible line.

I shift my weight.
One foot to the other.
Turn my head, always to the left,
never the right,

peering into the dusk
of that other world
where he paces—tall, thin, pale.
Beside me, but facing
the opposite direction.

I've hurt myself.
Pulled a muscle at waistline on my right side,
craning to see. Twisting
myself to search
the shape of his death.

I stretch to ease the pain.
I sit down. I put my right leg
across my left knee.
I lean forward. I feel the pull in my thigh.

Someone has imposed a screen
along the border between us.
A no man's land where all color is subtracted
save that of bruises.

Thus when I turn my head
he stands in a night that never truly
falls. His face ashen
above faded denim. Is it accusing,
stunned, or merely blank?

My own face is a mask.
It stares at me from the mirror.
In the morning I scrub it
with a soapy cloth. Rub cream
into it, around the eyes,
forehead, cheeks.
I apply gloss to its lips.

If I want to I can make it smile.

Winter Break at the Old Railroad Hotel

The fire's out in the wood stove
in the lobby, the switch on the lamp
is broken. Sleek bottles of cabernet,
merlot, Syrah, wrung
from these arid hills, gleam

from a locked cabinet.
The innkeeper and his wife
have gone home,
the chef takes Sundays off,
leaving us, the only guests,
with the door code and a number
to call if we need help.

Up and down the hallway
all the doors are locked.
We can roam the halls in our
night clothes, roll on the bed
in each other's arms,
make all the noise we want.
It is all ours—

the empty rooms, ghostly voices,
tramp of feet up the path
from the river, the yellow
eye of the lantern, creak
of the old ferry, sheep baaing
from the sheds by the dock.

Next day we cross the broken tracks,
walk the abandoned highway
wrapped in all the clothes we brought.
Wind rips the rimrock. It's so cold
my eyebrows hurt. Yellow lichen
dusts flat faces of basalt.
A chunk half the size of a car
lies in the middle of the road.

Ahead, three bald eagles hunch
in a gaunt tree. You take my hand,
warm it in your pocket. Two birds

lift off, soar in lazy
circles against the lucid sky.

Birds, Probably Birds

Waking this morning I thought of her,
and tonight walking the deck
to see the stars.

I'd see her driving past with groceries,
or last spring setting out primroses
in her newly spaded bed.

I thought of her lying in the river
not far from here, under the bridge.

The milky explosion when she landed,
the unbelievable silt.

And of the one who held her in his arms,

the trees bending down, the freshness of the air
above the earth's lung.

Birds, probably birds that morning,

as always. And probably the scent
on her skin, in her hair,
her limp body pressed against his chest,

recalled the briefest moment
of tenderness, a twitch

at the corner of his eye, before
he dropped her
into the river from the bridge

believing she would never be found.

The arc of the moral universe

that tends toward justice is so long
it bends over whole cities, villages,
over gas chambers, lime pits, over

stunned rooms in prison basements,
over the glare-light, the inquisitors'
serrated tools. Over shtetls,

huts, hooches, children whose lids
are clotted with flies,
over the sniper taking aim

at the girl who sells tulips
at market, over white-hooded men
with scissored eyes.

It bends over the grandmother
who rescues the slashed scrolls
from the rubble of the razed

Temple, rolls them in linen.
Over the black robes of eight judges,
from its source in the shattered stars.

Lazy Days

The dog has fleas,
cat too, kitchen faucet
rusted out, sink

clogged in the bathroom,
ice maker fizzled
on the hottest day.

Lucky me, and you too
if you possess such a list.
My laundry gentles

in the breeze, and I sit
with my feet up, the figs
on my tree oozing

sugar. I hear
in Palestine the Israelis
are bulldozing fig orchards

again, and olive groves.
I hear it's legal.
And necessary for the safety

of their people. But don't I
recall the Dresden Jew,
Victor Klemperer,

his diaries? There he sits
at a polished table,
his frayed cuffs, forced

to cede his house.
It was legal. He was
forbidden to keep a cat

anymore, a typewriter
or a car. His rations
were mainly potatoes.

He didn't own
a fig orchard, of course.
Or an olive grove.

1941:Escape

White dimity, starched linen,
    aprons embroidered,
        cross-stitched, smocked,

even those the smallest daughters
    wore (tiptoes on chair,
        fingers sprinkling almonds

into the strudel) one by one
    unfold themselves,
        slip from abandoned

cupboards. The sky
    is closing anyway,
        they feel it as certain animals

feel an impending quake.
    They gather in the park
        at dusk, a strange

fluttering white flock.
    The oldest call out
        they'll fly North,

over the sea. The youngsters
    tremble at going. Their calls
        echo the darkening sky.

View from the Porch

A hummingbird hovers
over the last few spectacular blooms
of crimson coreopsis,
which wave from the prow of a long
curved stem, itself
the very color of the dab and blur
of the bird's olive body.

Like a bee he tastes first one,
then the next, inserting
his wanton beak
into the vessel
of each delicate throat.

With burnished feet he grips
the frond's green lance,
displaying, in a startle
of light, the ruby gorget
at his throat, the ivory flash
at his elegant back.

In a sudden blur he rockets up,
launches himself
against the feathered missile
of an intruding hummer.

In a frenzy of aerial combat
he loops and twirls—
tiny airman—
proclaiming this is mine,

all mine, before he dives,
triumphant, to that last
isle of sweetness.

What I know about war

begins with a photo of my uncle
standing on a beach on Tarawa,
jabbing the tip of a Japanese sword
into a helmet
washed up at his feet like a ripe coconut,

and curving behind him,
a detonated shoreline, one lone palm
jagged in the distance,
at his feet wavelets licking his boots
like an afterthought,
and under the brim of his helmet,
eyes sun-blasted to shadow.

This is the man whose wife divorced him
in 1944, who never remarried,
or saw his son, the man
who appeared holidays only,
a twenty-pound bird under his arm,
and disappeared into the garage
with my father and a bottle,

who told me when I was seven
there was a *Jap head* inside that helmet.

The uncle who drove my 15-year-old self
to the corner market one Thanksgiving,
when the rain ran down the windshield,
and the wind pelted the trolley lines,
and last-minute shoppers hunched
under umbrellas in the parking lot,
fumbling for keys.

Who pulled from the glove box
a packet of photos of a naked woman,
splayed them like a deck of cards
in front of my eyes, then watched,
under the brim of his cap
for my reaction, as she aimed at me,
from inside the pinked edges
of the photo's frame,

the white torpedoes of her breasts,
the sticky pout of her lip-sticked mouth,
the dark wounds of her nipples.

Desecration

She snips Old Glory into little squares
as she sits beside his bed week
by week, stows them in a grocery bag,
stitches them back, one by one
to eight-patch squares.

When they prop him in his chair
his head hangs like a baby bird.
The white gauze, cinched tight
around his neck,
blinds the ordinary air.

The doctors skirt her chair.
They know by now a mother's grief.
And she knows their job's to keep
the kill-count down, keep
this war hidden from the public eye,
which is why,

on their first excursion out
to practice real life,
with three young aides, all smiles,
to help his dad and her
learn to care for him, she insists
to drape her patchwork flag across his knees.

Sitting at the restaurant table,
she tucks a cloth beneath his chin,
scoots close, as she used to do
before he knew his words.

That woman staring by the window—let her weep.

Pointing, one by one, she pronounces:
knife, spoon.

Already

as I swayed on my root-cord
in the vast inland sea
of my mother's womb,
U-boats prowled the Atlantic,
already my eye stalks
scanned the sea's depths,
already the buds of my limbs,
the jelly of my bones
prepared to resist their fire.

My teeth, my nails,
the silk of my hair already
rocked in their undersea
garden when bombers
a continent and ocean away,
over London, Berlin,
scuttled the skies. Already
the wings of the dead
a startle of birds
burst from the knife-ledge
of their one and only life.

The month of my birth
Iron Guardists shot the Jews
of Bucharest, boxcars
shuddered at crossings,
cracked open their doors.
Already Stalin's pact of folly
with Hitler blinkered,
and the locks on the gates
to the east were tricked,
when I slipped, a blonde-slicked,
winsome girl into this world,
and you ask
why I write poems of war.

Coop

Ruckus from the Barred Rock,
neck arched,
hopping down, cackling

her daily egg. Three
Jersey Reds dash
for a Silkie's prize worm.

Last week I saw
a songbird trapped
inside the cage, fluttering

high out of hen reach
on a beam beneath the roof,
until I shooed it out.

That afternoon my best hen—
the one with the white
ear patches who laid

the beautiful pearly eggs—
like the others
she loved to scratch a shallow

in the dirt, loll there
hottest summer days.
Guess she wasn't

quick enough. The others
pecked her body
bloody, left a heap

of wilted feathers in the dirt.
Not much is safe
from a clutch of hens.

This Life

Lying in bed this morning
I am grateful for the life
I've got—crouched
among the weeds, the sweet
suck as they rip from wet
soil. Colander in hand,
shucking fingers of peas.
And not some other life,
crammed in a boxcar,
crouched beneath the bombed
hull of a truck. Such a leisurely
life is my lot—a thick bowl
filling and emptying with ease
between sunrise and sunset.
Not standing in some scarred
field, searching for a sign,
a familiar plaid, a boot, flash
of skirt to say who was my own.

Arachnid

Dainty creature,
racing on her tippy toes,
down silken avenues,
to the wretched stinkbug
thrashing in her web.

Little sweetheart,
topaz sister,
see her stab her sabers,
inject bitter nectar,
retreat to her ambush
until her twitcher's dead.

Little seamstress,
little darling,
scuttles back to truss,
spins her silk *in situ,*
flips the bug like beefsteak,
wraps the shiny threads
round and round,
tacks them down.

See how she spruces,
tidies her twinkle toes,
a cat after carnage,
before she bustles back
to her swag.

Attaches her hawsers,
her buntlines, winches
by inches, bindle-wad
to love-leaf, canoodles
her swaddle
before she twigs up, spent.

The Same Old Sky
after a Miniature from an album by J. Petzki, 1620

Nature's always making a spectacle
of herself, flaunting her colors—

clouds rolling like Mozart curls
over the trees, that slight wisp of pink
painting an abalone sky—
in this long-ago scene by the river.

No sleight of hand needed
to fish the girl's cage from the lake,
where she's been dunked,
naked of course,
to teach her what's what.

No poppycock magician to make you laugh,
no jester to stand on his head.
Just that fat kid under the elm
lunching on bread and cider,
clapping his hands.

And those two pious old dudes in hats
who pull the girl's cage to the shore—
They're not staring, oh no!
At the pale peach of her breasts,
her nipples' white buds.

Oh God! It could be me in that cage—

always a sucker for a wink,
the click of a few coins on a hungry day.
Even for a hunk of cheese,
I'd have lifted my petticoats,
and run dab smack
into the dead fish of the law.

Oh well, as I say,
it was long ago. But *Always*
and *Ever* stain that sky.

Notes

Hunger, p. 2: This poem was inspired by the book "In Memory's Kitchen," edited by Cara De Silva and translated by Bianca Steiner Brown, published by Jason Aronson Inc. in 1996. *Krieg*, the German word for war, in the context of cooking, designates substitutions used for those ingredients that war had made scarce. Theresienstadt, also known as Terezin, was a World War II concentration camp located in Czechoslovakia.

Up Canyon from Maupin, p. 6: Maupin is a city in eastern Oregon on the banks of the Deschutes River.

Grief, p. 11: For David Williams, 6-25-1965 to 3-28-2010.

The arc of the moral universe, p. 14: First used in 1810 by Theodore Parker, the quote was most famously contained in a Baccalaureate sermon in 1964 by Martin Luther King.

Lazy Days, p. 15: Victor Klemperer, a German-Jewish scholar living in Dresden with his non-Jewish wife, Eva, was the author of two volumes of diaries, "I Will Bear Witness," together spanning the years 1933 to 1945.

1941:Escape, p. 16: This poem is a lyric attempt to imagine the desperate situation of the Jews in the spring and summer of 1941 in the Baltic States.

The Same Old Sky, p. 24: The Miniature referenced is labeled, "Fishing a harlot out of the river," and is accompanied by the following: "Prostitutes were known in Wroclaw from the Middle Ages. They had been carrying on their trade not only in brothels or on the streets, but also in bathhouses and cemeteries." The small book containing the copy of this miniature and others has been lost.

Dianne Stepp's poems have appeared in many literary journals and anthologies, including *High Desert Journal, TAMSEN, Cider Press Review, Comstock Review, Clackamas Literary Review, Windfall, Elohi Gadugi, Portland Lights,* and *Regrets Only.* She is a recipient of an Oregon Literary Arts Fellowship and a writer's residency at Caldera. Her first chapbook, *Half-Moon of Clay,* was published by Finishing Line Press in 2006. She is a graduate of the Warren Wilson MFA Program in Poetry, and is also a tapestry artist, spinner, teacher and avid gardener. A retired counselor, she lives in Portland, Oregon with her husband.

www.ingramcontent.com/pod-product-compliance
Lightning Source LLC
LaVergne TN
LVHW041557070426
835507LV00011B/1133